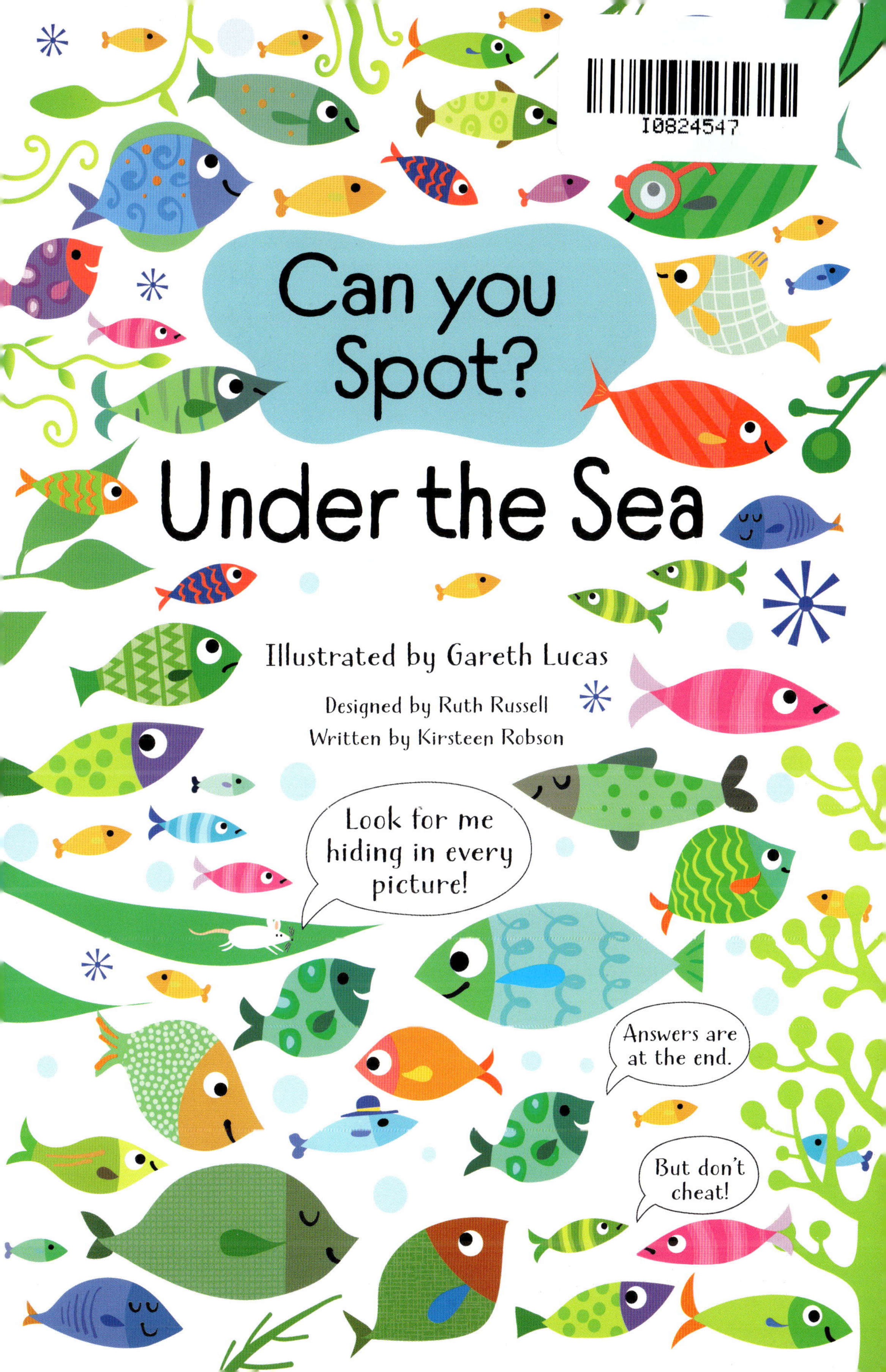
I0824547
Can you Spot?
Under the Sea
Illustrated by Gareth Lucas
Designed by Ruth Russell
Written by Kirsteen Robson
Look for me hiding in every picture!
Answers are at the end.
But don't cheat!

Spot a little blue crab.
Can you see a watch?
Can you spot...
3 pink shells like this
another toy diver

Who's wearing a hat?

2 other spotted fish

2 star earrings like this

3 more purple shells

Find three more flying fish like me.
Can you spot...
6 more gulls
2 other red oars

Can you see a wooden wheel?
Spot a bobbing boat.
another one of these
3 more groups of bright fish
another rubber ring

Who's got a bowl of noodles?
Which octopus has green eyes?
Can you spot...
another paper hat
5 more gold bracelets

Spot an octopus wearing socks.
6 other starfish
another 2 of these
3 octopuses just like this

Who has a spotted beak?
Can you spot...
2 more blue buckets
5 other dominoes

Can you see two yellow flippers?
Spot a penguin with tufty head feathers.
2 more of these
another toy penguin
1 more paper plane

Can you spot a broken pearl necklace?
Where's the key to the treasure chest?
Can you spot...
this crab's twin
6 other rings

Find a fish with a sparkly tiara on her head.
3 more of these
another golden cup
1 more fish like this

Who's wearing a life jacket?

Can you spot... another purple submarine 3 more bananas

Find a tiny yellow submarine.
Where did I hang the clothes on the line?
2 other fish like this
another paint brush
2 different cans of paint

Can you see
a crab riding
a dolphin?
Can you spot...
a shoe that
matches this one
2 more blue
bags

Which fish is wearing goggles?
Spot a bag with two handles.
another fish like this
1 more red shoe
2 other yellow balls

Have you seen my tooth that came out?
Who's got a purple fishing net?

Can you spot...

another little duckling

2 more of these

Where's my remote control?
3 other carrots
a fish just like this
another compass

Spot a fish
with a pirate's
eye patch.
Can you
see a swimming
parrot?
Can you spot...
3 more
pirates' hats
2 other seahorses
just like this

Find an old knife, fork and spoon.
another black flag
3 more starfish
2 other barrels

Who's wearing sunglasses?

Can you spot...

3 more goldfish

another 3 of these

Can you see a green crab?
Spot the shark who is asleep.
2 more toothbrushes
3 blue flags like this
1 other tube of toothpaste

Find two fish that match.

Where's my basket?

Can you spot...

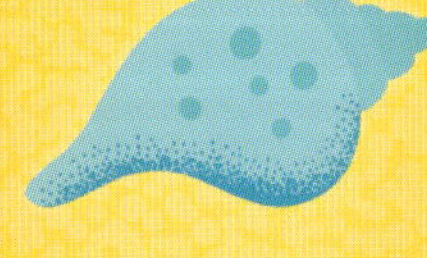

2 more blue shells

a shell that matches this

Which two seahorses are linking tails?
Spot three little orange fish.
Can you spot...
2 more ponies
another jellyfish, just the same

Help me find
a yellow fish.
Can you spot...
a snow shovel
like this
another
3 balls

Where's my other armband?
Can you spot three other seals?

3 more puffins

2 other pink fish

2 birds that match this one

Which turtle
is blowing shiny
bubbles?
Can you spot...
2 more
parrots
another 3
tomatoes

Look for a fish asleep in a hammock.
Who's wearing a mask?
a matching guitar
3 other palm trees
2 fish like this one

Have you seen a green sea snail?

Can you spot...

1 other watering can

1 more pink sunhat

Where have I left my beach towel?
Find a little yellow present.
2 bags the same as this
3 more pufferfish
another one of these

Answers

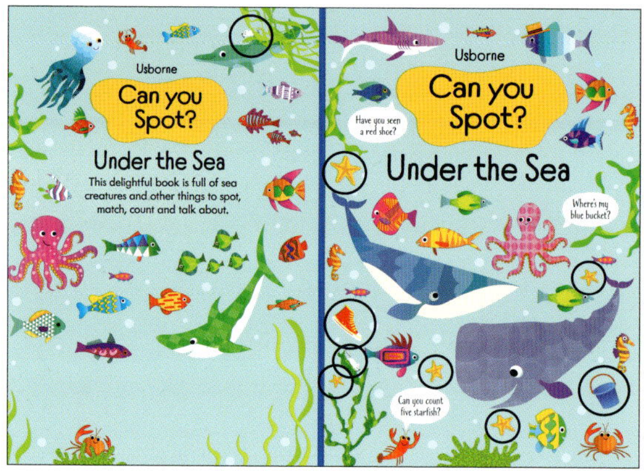
Usborne
Can you Spot?
Under the Sea
This delightful book is full of sea creatures and other things to spot, match, count and talk about.
Usborne
Can you Spot?
Under the Sea
Have you seen a red shoe?
Where's my blue bucket?
Can you count five starfish?

Cover

Spot a little blue crab.
Who's wearing a hat?
Can you see a watch?
Can you spot...
3 pink shells like this
another toy diver
2 other spotted fish
2 star earrings like this
3 more purple shells

2–3

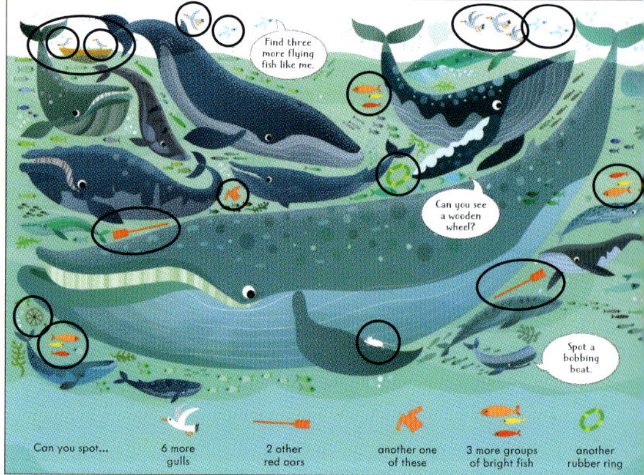
Find three more flying fish like me.
Can you see a wooden wheel?
Spot a bobbing boat.
Can you spot...
6 more gulls
2 other red oars
another one of these
3 more groups of bright fish
another rubber ring

4–5

Who's got a bowl of noodles?
Spot an octopus wearing socks.
Which octopus has green eyes?
Can you spot...
another paper hat
5 more gold bracelets
6 other starfish
another 2 of these
3 octopuses just like this

6–7

Can you see two yellow flippers?
Spot a penguin with tufty head feathers.
Who has a spotted beak?
Can you spot...
2 more blue buckets
5 other dominoes
2 more of these
another toy penguin
1 more paper plane

8–9

Can you spot a broken pearl necklace?
Where's the key to the treasure chest?
Find a fish with a sparkly tiara on her head.
Can you spot...
this crab's twin
6 other rings
3 more of these
another golden cup
1 more fish like this

10–11

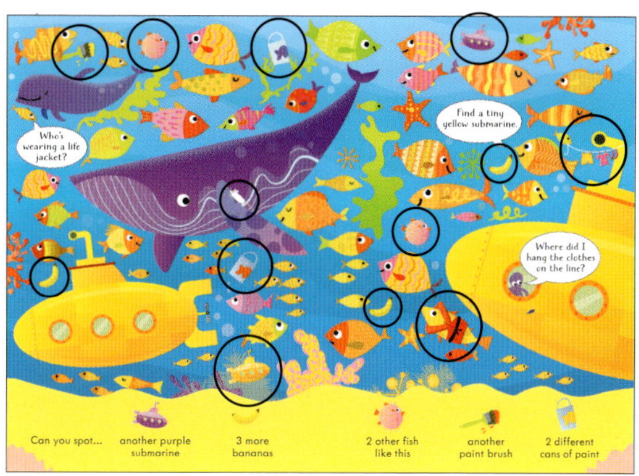
Who's wearing a life jacket?
Find a tiny yellow submarine.
Where did I hang the clothes on the line?
Can you spot...
another purple submarine
3 more bananas
2 other fish like this
another paint brush
2 different cans of paint

12–13

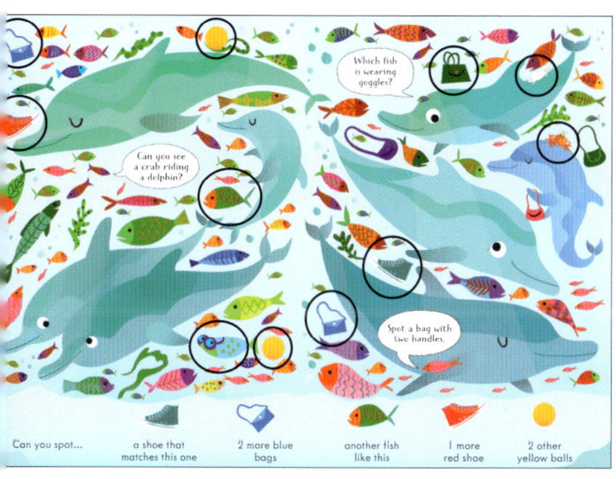
Which fish is wearing goggles?
Can you see a crab riding a dolphin?
Spot a bag with two handles.
Can you spot...
a shoe that matches this one
2 more blue bags
another fish like this
1 more red shoe
2 other yellow balls

14–15

Have you seen my tooth that came out?
Who's got a purple fishing net?
Where's my remote control?
Can you spot...
another little duckling
2 more of these
3 other carrots
a fish just like this
another compass

16–17

Spot a fish with a pirate's eye patch.
Find an old knife, fork and spoon.
Can you see a swimming parrot?
Can you spot...
3 more pirates' hats
2 other seahorses just like this
another black flag
3 more starfish
2 other barrels

18–19

Can you see a green crab?
Spot the shark who is asleep.
Who's wearing sunglasses?
Can you spot...
3 more goldfish
another 3 of these
2 more toothbrushes
3 blue flags like this
1 other tube of toothpaste

20–21

Find two fish that match.
Where's my basket?
Can you spot...
2 more blue shells
a shell that matches this
Which two seahorses are linking tails?
Spot three little orange fish.
Can you spot...
2 more ponies
another jellyfish, just the same

22–23

Help me find a yellow fish.
Where's my other armband?
Can you spot three other seals?
Can you spot...
a snow shovel like this
another 3 balls
3 more puffins
2 other pink fish
2 birds that match this one

24–25

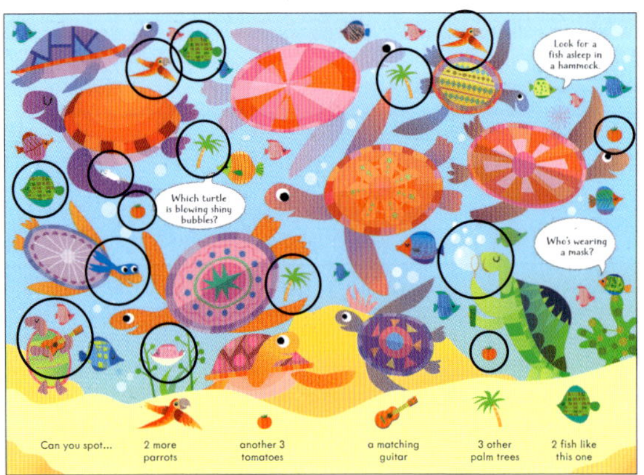
Look for a fish asleep in a hammock.
Which turtle is blowing shiny bubbles?
Who's wearing a mask?
Can you spot...
2 more parrots
another 3 tomatoes
a matching guitar
3 other palm trees
2 fish like this one

26–27

Where have I left my beach towel?
Have you seen a green sea snail?
Find a little yellow present.
Can you spot...
1 other watering can
1 more pink sunhat
2 bags the same as this
3 more pufferfish
another one of these

28–29

This edition first published in 2025 by Usborne Publishing Limited, 83–85 Saffron Hill, London EC1N 8RT, United Kingdom. usborne.com UE. This edition first published in America 2025. Printed in China.